LABOR DAY FUN

cOLORING book for all ages

By Beauty In Books

About the Author

"Aby Sparklewood is an accomplished author with a unique talent for crafting captivating children's fiction and insightful business books. With a playful imagination and a keen business sense, her stories ignite young minds and inspire entrepreneurs to reach new heights of success."

ENGINEERS

Sanitation Workers

Postal Workers

Farmers

Grocery Store Workers

POLICE OFFICERS

TEACHERS

NURSE

FIRE FIGHTERS

SOCIAL WORKERS

CONSTRUCTION WORKERS

WAREHOUSE WORKERS

ELECTRICIAN

AIR TRAFFIC CONTROLLER

EMERGENCY DISPATCHER

Check out my other books by
Scanning the QR code or using
the link below

linktr.ee/beautyinbooks3